DEFLECTION

DEFLECTION

Poems by
Roberta Beary

Accents Publishing • Lexington, Kentucky • 2015

Printed in the United States of America

Accents Publishing
Editor: Katerina Stoykova-Klemer
Cover Art: *Thaw* by Kevin Beary

ISBN: 978-1-936628-33-9
First Edition

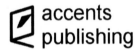

accents
publishing

Accents Publishing is an independent press for brilliant voices. For a catalog of current and upcoming titles, please visit us on the Web at

www.accents-publishing.com

For Frank

CONTENTS

57 VARIETIES

it's not the worst thing she's ever done.
it's not one of her better moments either.
she lists her reasons.
but i don't hear them. i don't have to.
i know for her the switch is off.
the one that always used to be on.
no matter what he says, what he does.
she's lost her taste for him.
he's like that ketchup bottle.
the one she keeps for show.

in and out of *weeds* bingeing on netflix

AFTERGLOW

rose petal saké—
my crazy is not
his crazy

jasmine scent of the other woman is me

daymoon
grass stains
of original sin

broken vow the gin bottle's vacant blue

the way he says
consensual
mauve sunset

AROUND HERE

things are starting to slip. the daily dog walk is a flat-out lie as
is any form of exercise. personal grooming is more goal than
reality. witness madprofessor eyebrows and stray nose hairs.
everywhere are dusty stacks of expired energy drinks. that no
one is willing to toss.

at least not just yet.

mother sleeps
on and off
we talk hospice

BEFORE THE OUTING

i

my son's boyfriend
three words i practice saying
alone in my room

ii

rainbow flag
father pretends
not to see

iii

not something
that's contagious
still you step back
from my son
and his boyfriend

iv

rainbow flag
mother tiptoes around
the subject

v

with knife in hand
my son's lover dissects
the last white peach

BONSAI GALLERY

chinese quince
the one who left me
never left

fullmoon maple a lie of omission

scarlet katsura
we exchange
past lives

needle juniper my dna on your pocket comb

pomegranate
no way to read
our future

BRINGING UP BABY

again she falls. but nothing's broken and she seems okay.
still i go a little crazy. i look for a nurse. then grab my phone.
the big screen is turned up super loud. as usual.
she tells me to be quiet and points at the movie.
an old black and white. screwball comedy, circa 1938.
she says hush! then puts her finger to her lips
just in case i don't get the message.
my daughter, serene at 25, gives me one of her knowing looks.
grandma's fine she says. she sits down right next to her.
side by side their faces edge toward the screen.
they laugh at the same parts. when baby surprises cary grant.
or gets a big kiss from kate hepburn.
i watch the two of them on the loveseat.
my own private screening.
heads so close together
there's no room for me.

mockingbird song turning from day to dusk

CARETAKER—I

florida sunshine
mother soaks up
the shade

cherry blossoms
the incessant sound
of mother's cough

mother's day
only the tulips
come calling

in the wheels
of mother's chair
wet leaves

cheshire moon
mother no better
no worse

autumn moon
her brain a tangle
of white string

winter solstice
no spark of recognition
in mother's brown eyes

blue crocus
mother will never
get better

CARETAKER—II

rain all day
a place i cannot reach
in mother's eyes

hospice day
a flutter of movement
in mother's hand

resurrection sky
mother somewhere between
here and there

bone dry
mother's hand
in mine

brief sunset
a world beyond this one
in mother's eyes

day of blossoms
a nurse erases
mother's name

forsythia
the funeral
unfolds

on the church steps
a mourning dove
with mother's eyes

DEFLECTION

mother gone
my urgent need
for a new coat

tai-chi rain
all my weight on
the wrong foot

radiant heat
one free upgrade
to orphan

white christmas
a black line
for my signature

birdsong
of vocal dystonia—
tea for one

DEMENTIA (MILD TO MODERATE)

My mother hugs me hard and tells me I am beautiful. She says, "I love you, I love you" in a voice that anyone can hear. She blows kisses my way. We hold hands and she turns her head and smiles at me. When I get up to leave, she asks me to stay for dinner. She grins and says there is a man she wants me to meet, someone who adores her. I demur and say I have to leave. She laughs, then says, "I won't hold it against you!" In my life, I have never known her to be cheerful. I have never seen her engage in banter. Or dish out compliments. I do not know this woman. I want my mother back.

long after ...
the frailty
of silk roses

FERRY CROSSING

ticket line
a blue dragonfly
invades my space

inside a wide mirror spirits for sale

whale sighting
my gender
also unknown

starboard a butterfly out of context

gull after gull
the changing color
of sky

dockside a sailor anchors summer's end

FREE-FLOATING

my heartbeat wakes me. it's 2 a.m. is the baby okay? i run to
check. the baby's room is empty.

my eyes scan the compass points: north, no white crib; east,
no changing-table; south, no goodnight moon; west, no mister
bear.

my mind computes. a few years back we turned the baby's room
into my study. it seemed so important once. i can't remember
why.

dead of night
thoughts the lamplight
illuminates

IRISH TWINS

We share an attic room.
In the corner is an old double bed
that smells and sags on one side. My side.
Late at night I hear my heart beat. Loud.
So loud he will hear it. He will think my heart
is calling him up the attic stairs.
His footsteps are heavy.
He smells of old spice
and cherry tobacco.
My eyes shut tight.
I know he is there.
I feel his weight.
Never on my side.
Always on the side she sleeps.
When the bedsprings sing their sad song
I fly away. Up to the ceiling. My sister is already there.
Together we hold hands. Looking down we see our bodies.
We are not moving. We are as still as the dead.

attic rain
the backyard swing
off-kilter

JOURNAL ENTRY / JANUARY 1

1) practice patience. (in italian it's patienza.)

2) relearn italian.

3) find in the house (check attic, closets, and basement) all 3 editions of *oggi in italia* including:
   a) half-finished workbooks &
   b) cassette tapes.
   (note to self: does anyone listen to tapes besides me?)

4) who am i kidding? note to self: you know it is: whom am i kidding? don't get off topic.

5) this is too hard—throw everything out:
   i) textbooks—all 3 editions;
   ii) workbooks (w/n finished);
   iii) cassette tapes. (really do this, do not put anything back— use outside garbage can, not inside one!)

6) find top 3 online italian courses.

7) read all course reviews by real people only.

8) compare (italian) course prices.

9) put all info on spreadsheet ...
   (if needed ask for help. in italian it's aiutatemi!)

10) practice patience.

first light
a paper rose unfolds
the new year

LAST RITES

chest pains
breathing in
the sunset

hospice bed
the get-well roses
stunted bloom

thin sunlight
eyelids flutter
in morphine sleep

deathwatch
the arrival of fresh
coffee

day moon
we windowshop
caskets

day of the obit
inside his wallet
me at eleven

LIPSTICK

pity the daughters of beautiful mothers
the years spent waiting to grow
into a beauty that never comes
the sympathetic looks
finally understood at the moment
when childhood ends

mother's visit
side by side we outline
our lips

MEMORARE

May is the month of Mary every day in May
be sure to wear something blue in Mary's honor
that never was it known that anyone who fled
to thy protection implored thy help or sought
thy intercession was left unaided patent leather
shoes are not allowed because boys must be
kept free from temptation *to thee do I come*
before thee I stand sinful and sorrowful always
remember your guardian angel *despise not my*
petitions but in thy mercy hear and answer me

meth addict
the baby face
in my wallet

NIGHTHAWKS

tonight her breathing's more shallow. i try to find her favorite
songs. search quickly on my iPad. *mack the knife* by Bobby;
replays of Vera's *we'll meet again*. but mostly i just talk and she
listens. eyes glued shut in coma-land. well past morning i kiss
her rice-paper face. stroke her white hair. a voice is crying,
calling mama, mama. a word back from dead. executed in the
land of assimilation. just after noon mama curls in fetal position.
i keep watch: rise and fall of out-of-breath beats. too soon it
comes. ebb tide.

autumn coolness enters a hand long held in mine

ON THE F TRAIN

reading the copy of howl
you gave me years ago on some
birthday a tote bag filled
with all the poetry books
it could hold and when you left me
all the books a little worse for wear
but the tote bag still intact

old subway car
the cane seat's
broken weave

PHILANTHA

we never had a child
together
we used to talk about it
sometimes
when it was still
a possibility
what color hair
whose eyes
that kind of thing
we never got
as far as names

home again
driveway daffodils
come and gone

SNOW BIRD

sandpiper shore
the shell-seeker's
rooted stance

I was 15.
He was older and here all year.
Even summers.
His name is lost.
His face a blur.
Blue letters on a white board say,
"Private - No Trespass."
But I do.

My toes feel the silky weave.
Of the net he cast.
I know what was caught.
And released.

SUMMERTIME BLUES

suddenly single—
a carpenter bee gives me
the wrong kind of buzz

midday-haze
after the tune up
still out-of-tune

overripe no one to mow my lawn

4th of july
the couples
all ginned up

finality defined
all the dog day
afternoon

can't shake it off heat lightning

SUNDAY DINNER

i like my husband but not the older sister
too bossy for me the way she likes
to tell me we don't call him sweetie pie
in this house who died and made her
queen and the younger sister too
always talking money and how poor
growing up but mostly i don't like
the way they knew him
all those stolen years
before he found me

porch-glider
the rosethorns
back and forth

THE OFFER

Squirrels in the attic. As soon as I walk in the door, I hear them. Inside the walls. Screeching a code I can't break. Right on cue he asks me to move back. If I do, he'll call someone. About the squirrels. I promise, he says. His eyes get watery. Like he's trying not to cry.

coffee percolating away the rest of my life

He's says he's old. He no longer can take care of himself. I take a good look. He needs a shave. He needs a haircut. He needs a wash. This man who used to scare me to death.

The squirrels get louder. Quick, he says, his heavy cane raised. Bang. Bang. Bang. So hard a crack forms on the ceiling. God damn you to hell, he says. Look what you made me do. I need to get something, I say. In my car.

rear-mirror the stunted pine's red robin

It was the squirrels, calls a voice from the doorway. Not you. Come back inside, says the voice. Come back.

WHAT REMAINS

What are you thinking when you drive at midnight on a lonely stretch of highway? When you look down at your phone? When your fingers find the keypad and type out: *c u l 8 r*? When you hit "send"? Do you think we will not weep for you?

> support group
> sunlight moves across
> empty faces

I always thought we would have time to repair the old grievances. I never thought I would be the recipient of your story told over and over. Words that never change: "Imagine losing your only son. Imagine." What remains after the words are gone?

> a blue cat roams
> the empty hours ...
> cold winter moon

You leave us with one last story. It is 4 o'clock in the morning. A police car sets its revolving light on a mother's house. The shadow of two men appears. The front door opens. One man is a policeman. This is where the story ends. The other man is a priest. This is where the story begins.

ACKNOWLEDGMENTS

Thanks to the editors and publishers of the following journals in which versions of these poems first appeared: *Acorn, Atlas Poetica (Chiaroscuro—25 LGBT Tanka), cattails, frogpond, haijinx, Lilliput Review, Mariposa, Modern Haiku, Moonset, NOON: journal of the short poem, Notes from the Gean, The Heron's Nest, tinywords, Upstate Dim Sum,* and *Valley Voices.*

Prior to publication in *Deflection* versions of some of the poems were reprinted in two anthologies. "Irish Twins," "Memorare" and "Nighthawks" were reprinted in the anthology *Journeys: An International Anthology of Haibun* (Nivasini Publishers, India 2014.) "Afterglow" and "Nighthawks" were reprinted in the anthology *fear of dancing* (Red Moon Press, 2014.) "Bringing Up Baby" was posted in the webzine *Ink Sweat & Tears* on May 23, 2013. The haiku in the haibun "Lipstick" is used with permission of Snapshot Press.

Special thanks to senior editor Katerina Stoykova-Klemer and editor Christopher McCurry of Accents Publishing for their skillful supervision in the production of this book.

With gratitude to my family for their love and support: daughter Nina, son Nathan, and husband Frank.

CPSIA information can be obtained at www.ICGtesting.com
Printed in the USA
LVOW11s0920250315

431911LV00001B/4/P

9 781936 628339